HEL

Also by Elizabeth Burns

HELD

ELIZABETH BURNS

First published in Great Britain in 2010 by Polygon,
an imprint of Birlinn Ltd
West Newington House
10 Newington Road
Edinburgh
EH9 1QS
www.birlinn.co.uk

ISBN: 978-1-84697-170-9

British Library Cataloguing-in-Publication Data
A catalogue record for this book is available on request
from the British Library.

Typeset by Koinonia, Manchester
Printed and bound by Bell & Bain Ltd., Glasgow

Acknowledgements

Some of these poems have appeared in the following magazines and anthologies:

And the Story Isn't Over (poetry pf, 2009), *Artemis, Artesian, Assent, The Dark Horse, Fras, The Interpreter's House, island, Markings, Northwords Now, Scintilla, Skeins of Geese* (The Shed Press, 2008), *Tears in the Fence, Tenemos, Textualities, The Warwick Review, Watermark* (Flax Books, 2006) and *Zed 2 O*.

The sequence 'The shortest days' was published as a pamphlet by Galdragon Press (2008) and won the 2009 Michael Marks Award for Poetry Pamphlets.

'Holy water' was commissioned by Shore Poets as the 2009 Mark Ogle Memorial Poem.

Contents

The journey home

Held

Held

One year old, and he's discovering the river,
dropping stones in at the edge, retrieving them.

He loves containers, says his mother,
then wonders, is a river a container?

The riverbed is: it curves its way from Roeburndale
down through these woods of wild garlic and bluebells,

letting the winding stony vessel of itself be filled
with springwater, meltwater, rainwater,

water which also contains things – you can plop
a stone into it, take it out again,

and here are glints of fish and floating twigs,
silt, insects, air-bubbles, ducklings –

and if the river's a container, so's a song,
holding words and tune; an eggshell

holds a bird, the atmosphere
enfolds the planet; everything is like a basket

says the basketmaker, the earth contains us,
we contain bones, blood, air, our hearts.

We are baskets and makers of baskets,
and fresh from the hold of the womb

the boy-child's discovering how things
are held by other things: milk in a cup,

food in a bowl, a ball in his hands,
a stone in water, water in a nest of stones.

Shakespeare does the cross-bay walk

Why? Because he could, because the sands were there,
a pale flat sheet pulled out between the strong arms
of the bay, like a washerwoman's laundry;
and what was seabed is uncovered, laid bare
and fresh, untouched. Its huge wingspan.
His bare feet squelch in sand. He feels the pull of it
around his ankles; plods on; one foot heaved out
and then the other. Then a flowing current, clear water
washing caked mud off his skin. He sees the ghost
of hoofprints fading in wet sand, the hollows
made by other travellers' boots filling now
with seawater: these little pools, these new-formed landscapes
that we make as our footsteps take us over earth.
The land ahead, the shining cloth that leads to it –

and then he's deep in, up to his knees, he sees himself drawn down,
sinking, mouthfuls of sand: all the words he's yet to speak
and write stopped in his throat. And why?
Because he wanted to discover how it felt
to walk across the sea, become amphibious, a man
turned seal or otter – and he cannot. He yanks his feet up,
grabs his neighing horse's belly like a raft, pulls himself
onto the creature's back. It sways, drags up soaked fetlocks,
staggers to a sand bar. They falter on, man and horse;
they'll cross the bay by nightfall, feel flat unmoving land
under them again. The horse, rubbed down, will eat its oats
and sleep. And he – he will relish being human, not webbed
or gilled, but here, splayed feet on solid ground,
the tongue inside his mouth not bound by sand.

Vessel

Here is where they laid her,
lifeless, in a bed of stone

carved to her body's shape.
There was a covering once,

some kind of lid, long gone,
and in the space her body filled

there's only sea air,
a puddle of rainfall,

spray from a high tide.
There may have been earth

in the emptied grave shape
and grass, a few harebells –

or fire, an offering to a god
made over flames of driftwood

kindled in the cold stone
that holds a memory

of hands held round a bowl
and people supping food together.

Horse

A horse takes shape on a hillside.
It is three thousand years ago.

They are drawing the lines
of its body, digging and lifting

the skin of turf, exposing
the white flesh of earth

which buries its secrets
deep, has in its keeping

bones, flints, vessels,
beads for spindle-whorls,

hearth-stones,
the grave-place of a child;

until time comes to carefully
shift the soil, begin to sift

and piece together fragments
of a story, making

– as we on earth have always done –
something whole from what is

broken, separate:
mud and fire that make the pot,

chalk and grass the horse,
still galloping over the hill.

Trench

An iron-age camp on the Ridgeway
mapped in green and red inks:

cross-sections, elevations
and everywhere circles

– hillforts, roundhouses,
storage pits, grave mounds –

but the trench is a rectangle
marked off with string:

a segment of earth
whose layers are being peeled back

as carefully as the restorer's hand
lifts off a skin of crackled varnish,

revealing what is underneath,
however smudged and shadowed.

Trench – its depths and angles measured,
the content of its soil defined –

gives up its history, but something's
always blurred or not quite straight:

the furtive curves and circles
that whirl and spiral over the earth.

History

It's seventy years since the last chunks of sandstone
were hauled down to the shore and set in concrete,
lozenges of stone with rose or ochre strata
fixed into a sea wall that slopes up from the beach
towards a field where horses graze and lapwings nest
and medieval drains push through eroded earth.

Of the abbey, what remains are bumpy outlines
– cloisters, nave, infirmary – and the squat, rounded
chapterhouse, its shape echoed by, dwarfed by,
the power station just up the coast, whose indestructible
waste is in the seabed where layers of sediment
became the quarried sandstone, heaved over salt marsh

to be turned into an abbey: a busy little world that lasts
four hundred years, till dissolution cracks it apart,
and the walls, like skin around the soul, fall away,
tumbled into the mossfield, from where the broken,
consecrated stone is laden into boats, rowed across
the estuary, made into houses on a village street

and the bell that used to measure out the days is looted,
melted down, its metal sold for cannonshot.
Monks have no descendants, but the ghosts of those
who died here of the plague are said to wander
in a nearby garden; and if one of these spirits were to visit
this windswept shoreline again, perhaps he'd find it

much as it once was, lapwings feeding in the grass
dotted pink and yellow with cranesbill and tormentil.
Take him on into another century, and maybe what he'll see
is the shell of the power station, decommissioned,
and the sea wall helpless, unable to prevent waves
swamping wildflowers, or creeping under the door

of the chapterhouse, covering with saltwater
its old carved gravestones. Here, in this moment
of history, the memory of a bell is chiming in his head
and he has a sense, like something pulled up from a dream,
that once, behind him in that field, there was a building
whose walls were lit pink-gold on evenings like this.

An eighteenth-century experiment

If you were to scoop a cup of water up,
here where the river mingles with the sea,
freshwater, saltwater twisting over rocks,
could you tell if the droplets were those

which had travelled down the valley
from the hills, knowing only silty, pebbly
river bed, bearing only twigs, fish, leaves,
perhaps the carcass of a sheep?

Would you know if this were water from the ocean
brought here by the rush of estuary
as it shoves itself inland, a high tide deep enough
to bring a slave-ship right up to the quayside?

Could you tell if this were water which had floated
one of those well-built vessels, its hold full
of sugar, cotton, chocolate and mahogany,
or glass beads and whisky, or human beings?

Could you tell which were the drops that formed the waves
that held the bloated bodies of those thrown overboard?
Or is this simply water from the hills,
clear and cold as a spring?

And another question: if you were to break
two eggs – one brown, one white – into a bowl,
could you tell from either of the golden yolks
what was the colour of its shell?

Transport

Because the barges were laden with gunpowder
the horses pulling them were shod with copper
so that no spark from their hooves could ignite
the explosives on their way to the seaport.

Past rosehips and willows and water lilies
they travelled, the kegs so delicately
handled, holding their powder of saltpetre
and charcoal and the ash of kelp which crofters

had gathered into sacks on beaches of white sand;
these gently rolled barrels carried in the holds
of cargo ships, and bushels of the sulphury stuff
unloaded, carefully, lids prised off,

grains measured out. Across the other side of ocean,
soft black powder, the moment of explosion.

The kennel

She reads the book over and over, she is travelling
through the story of a Jewish girl escaping Germany,
trying to make sense of the world and the war
that her grandparents lived through.

Her innocence – she reads *Hitler* as *Hilter*,
mispronounces *Nazis* – is falling away.
The part that she tells to her sister,
which it seems they can scarcely believe,

is about a professor kept in a kennel
chained up by the gate of the camp.
He goes mad. The little one asks,
how did they attach the chain, was it round his neck?

This question is inside the children now,
making a space for itself among stories
and worries and terrible facts. Pieces
of their memories are given over to these things

and have to be: amnesia, the blackout curtain,
would be worse. They have to carry with them
this bag of stones, these rattling marbles in their heads,
remembering and repeating; not forgetting, not repeating.

Poem for an elective mute

for a child who has already learned the power
of silence, and folds it round her like a cloak,

who lives in quietude
as does a Quaker or an angler or a nun,

who knows there is too much
clamour and chatter in the world

and to whom I offer
images of things which are moving

yet so silent that only the pipistrelle
might hear them:

the baby hovering in the womb,
snowfall, or the flight of swallows,

a new moon, not yet visible,
once called the silent moon,

the artist in her studio – *I can't talk
when I paint and it's very quiet* –

the petals of the white rose as they open
and as they fall; and all the words

which fly around her head, not ready
to alight yet on her tongue –

In the butterfly house

Butterflies are landing on the potter's cheeks,
his neck and forehead, they are tickling his skin,
batting his eyelashes with their wings.

One lands on his finger: he passes it on to his son
who perhaps feels the touch of it the way he feels
music alight on the string of his guitar

and the girl whose head is full of poems
cups in her hands a butterfly whose wing
is broken, and keeps that image in her head

while her sister looks at the velvet of wings
whose colours she will see days later
in the print of an iris, its blue-black inks,

and the boy thinks how his sister's fingers
flit lightly over the piano, as if in flight,
and how their friend would write a story

about someone going out without knowing
that a butterfly's clinging to their coat,
and outside it has started to snow –

Not yet teenagers, but already they are learning the creative life,
how hard it is: practice, revision, remaking,
trying to give shape to what's inside your head, waiting

for the idea, waiting for the work to come right,
for the notes to sound pure, for the colour to be perfect,
the poem to scan, the story to flow and be resolved.

They all know how this feels, though they don't – or can't –
speak of it to each other: they are simply children
throwing a frisbee or running downhill in the wind,

drinking hot chocolate, kicking a ball, but in each of them,
the particular gift, the thing that *makes you ache with happiness*,
in each of them the damp and crumpled wings unfurling.

Her metamorphosis

Evening sun in the plum blossom – the lit tree
white, gold, haloed – but you'd look at it later.
Later the sun disappeared, later it rained,
the blossom fell. No more light on petals,
the tree is all leaf now, a different creature,

just as your daughter, in flux, is blossoming,
opening – impossible not to take this image,
as old as myth or story, but add to it this:
that while the young girl is transformed,
her mother is, fleetingly, looking away.

Kathleen in Silloth

This is where he brings her: to the furthest tip
of England. This will be her married life.

She's Mrs Wilson here in Silloth,
the 'Ferrier' buried deep inside her.

She does the shopping, gives piano lessons,
invites the neighbours round for tea and cake

and perhaps a little Schumann. In summertime
the trippers come, and she gives the odd recital.

The Solway tides ease in and out, the surface
of the sea is calm. This beach does not have breakers.

She practices her scales. They ripple out into the quiet streets
and this feels enough like sanity, the way her hands

move on the keyboard. But on occasion
when the house is empty, she finds herself

singing in her old contralto, the voice
her mother thought too loud, too like a man's.

Sometimes at night she goes down to the shore
where the flat sea rustles over shingle

and flings that voice across the sea to Scotland.
She feels it like an animal inside her, crouched

and velvet-pawed, waiting in its cage.
It's fiercer in her than the playing of piano –

those scales and minuets all fall away.
She knows this thing, this song,

that claws about inside her like a tiger or a bear,
can't be contained much longer.

She's playing piano at the competition in Carlisle
when she hears the sound of singing from the next-door room

and her own voice gnaws at her throat.
She sets it loose, it fills the hall, it turns their hearts,

she wins the prize: her life begins. That night
she goes down to the shore and feels the soft wind

blowing and lets the cool air fill her lungs,
and then her voice takes flight, some great bird now

she sees it as – an osprey or an eagle
with its wings unbound, soaring up into the night sky

and out towards the ocean and the places
where the crashing breakers are colossal.

The shortest days

i.m. DGB and PGH

The enfolding

As the potter enfolds air with porcelain,
making, in this new vessel,

a presence round an absence,
containing what's invisible

and at the same time smoothing into being
something that the hands can cup,

so, walking though October woods
I find myself reaching out

in some ancient gesture
of holding and encircling

as if I clasped my hands
around your body in its sickness –

as if by this I could give you,
for a moment, strength,

fastening more tightly
your spirit to its fragile skin.

Beautiful mind

The things inside his mind are blurring
and drifting like snow, they are settling
into great heaps, burying whatever lay there.
May there be moments that feel as if they were lifted
from his granddaughter's collage of autumn:

the three pairs of pale gold sycamore wings, perhaps,
with their flying birdshapes echoing one another;
the bend and swoop and line of reddened leaf-stems,
or else the copper beech leaves, so exactly placed,
the white space clear between them, perfect as snow.

The shortest days

How the low sun flamed on those afternoons
with their early dusks, how the crusts of snow
in the pasture cast their blue shadows

and the moon's shape grew sharper,
land and sky just prised apart
by the horizon's slit of paler light

like the way the colours meet in *Black on Grey*,
that luminescence, thread of light, so fine
it's scarcely visible: the shred of a life

that's almost swallowed up
by dark. His last days on earth:
the precious lightness of his breath.

The wave

How his thinned face resembled his mother's
How his voice became a whisper barely heard

How his breath grew shallower and came no more
like a low wave disappearing into sand

How he seemed then like a shadow,
something that had been solid and substantial

laid out flat: an outline, an absence
like darkened sand where a wave has been

Last

Late summer, and the last of daylight
grows more precious: it's as if by gazing at the sky
I could somehow bear the sunset's weight,
keep back the dark that comes so quickly

and, scattering the ashes in the field at dusk,
I don't look down at the earth where they fall
but keep my eyes fixed on the sky,
the last of the light, its yellow so pale.

At Carstairs Junction

Something makes me glance up as we pass
the river, the one that floods the fields so easily,
where wind is rippling the grass like green silk.
A shimmer of memory: getting ready to alight,
the river telling us that we were almost there,
and that you would be waiting on the platform
of the station where this train no longer stops.

The arrival

I dream that the woman in the horse-drawn cart
is being pulled into a dark lake flecked with stars,
but she's ready to go, she lets the horse lead her

deep into that cold, enfolding water and those of us
who watch her go speak one word: *advent*.
I wake to the sound of the phone and the news

of your death in the night. Later, as instructed
in the dream, I look up the meaning of the word
and find *a coming, an arrival*.

The scales

And if there were some way to take the weight
of all your sorrow, heavy as wet sand,
I would do it: our lives are tipped scales,
mine all air and weightlessness, yours leaden.

But these moments when I think of you
and a sense of your loss pours through me –
are they, like some form of prayer,
a shouldering of your heaviness,

a time when the grains of sea-sand shift
and you feel, so briefly, lightness again?

White

Almost the last thing he made in this life
was the collage in white:
a still-life abstracted to texture

and shape, gradations of shade,
as if it had gathered into itself
all the colour-soaked world;

everything he had absorbed
pared down to a whiteness
like that of the masses of narcissi

all swaying in the wind
or the wings of the whooper swans
rising over the estuary

or this bowl made of porcelain,
its rim so fine
the white becomes translucent.

The colour of water

This keepsake, your sketchbook
of Orkney, has pencil drawings of the sea
annotated with soft, northern tones:
'steel grey', 'light blue', 'pale mauve'.

If I could have brought you something back
from Canada, it would have been the memory
of the colours of the lakes and rivers there,
the words for them, 'deep turquoise', 'milky green'.

This would have been your gift. Instead,
a sense of something missing,
like water lifted from its element
and running through my fingers, colourless.

Eulogy

A eulogium for you would be woven
from the honey-coloured haze of willow
on the marshland where I walked
with your widow, the path by the river
so familiar it was as if you were there
among the willows with us, a presence

like the scent of primrose or narcissus
hanging in the soft West Country air
that would fill the empty space
inside your willow sphere.

The journey home

The journey home

Full of delays, like a slow-motion dream, it will take all day,
yet somehow this seems necessary, a way of lengthening
the distance, lessening the jolt as you move from one world
to another; away from the house where he lived, where all week
he's been remembered, talked about; invisible yet present
like the flooded grass of these fields. But you can never
turn back now and see him waving as you leave.
Moving slowly homewards through this day of buses, trains,
icy stations, sandbagged backstreets, fallen trees,
raw January wind, you come to a muddy river still in spate
and cross its bridge towards your ordinary life, its solitary grief,
as Orpheus, returning empty-handed from the underworld
and knowing he would only ever see the dead in dreams,
crossed the river and began his journey home.

Fog

The morning of Christmas Eve, the fog so thick
it seems like a thing you could take in your hand,
so cold it shocks your lungs. You wade through it,
become invisible as you cross the pasture,

climb to the ghosted row of beech trees
then make your way towards the railway track.
There are no distances, the hills are swallowed up,
you see only what is close – rime on barbed wire,

frozen crusts of mud, the latch gate
that leads to the tracks. The sound of a train
comes muffled and damped, its yellow headlamps
pushing through fog, and then gone.

You pass the lake with its film of ice,
then head for the field where the horses graze,
and stare into the blurry whiteness, trying
to make them out. Something emerges

and here they come, galloping, six of them, seven, eight –
crossing the field from one side to the other,
vanishing back into fog, as if they were shadows
of horses, a dream of horses, breathing their strangeness

over Christmas, a gift, like the tree at the gate,
dripping with frosted crabapples.
Things that appear out of fog – fruit, light, glitter,
creatures, an illuminated face, your father's,

two Christmases ago, his last bright lucid moment
as he listened to his grandchild sing – brief as the frost
that will melt, brief as the fog itself that will lift,
but which today is what surrounds us, is our air.

Song for Claudia

It is Easter morning, and raining, but the table
is bright with flowers and blown eggs,
their gold paint glinting in candlelight
and we are eating Easter bread,
the oval loaf you've sent us from Germany,
bread that you make every year
from your grandmother's recipe
so that the kneading reminds you of her
and of your mother, who also made it,
piercing the dough as Christ was pierced,
filling the holes with egg yolk and sugar
so the loaf is studded with circles of yellow
like little suns. Tucked in the parcel,
a letter, your memories of my father.
The biscuits you sent us at Christmas
arrived the day that he died, and we ate them,
crumbly and almondy, with hot milk or tea
on those bitterly cold afternoons.

There was a winter morning years ago – our first
shared birthday – when we breakfasted together,
the table full of bread and flowers, the day
not yet light, snow falling at the window.
'Star sisters' you call us, born the same day of the year,
the day that we phone, or send letters and cards;
one year, a lantern you'd made from waxed paper,
its candle each Christmas casting a pattern of stars
round our room, as your own lantern does
on the pale golden walls of your flat in Berlin.

It is Easter morning, and raining, and the children
will hunt a wet garden for eggs, and we'll come in
to coffee, and more of your yellow-flecked bread,
warm in our mouths with the promise of spring.

Brave new world

Emerging from the cracked dark chrysalis of wartime
with its underground shelters, blacked-out windows,
you shake out adolescent wings and fly in light and air –

The world's expanding: anything seems possible.
Flush with youth, you're poised on the edge of an age
whose optimism will define your life.

The first thing, your pen-pal in Holland – a line of ink
that links you, lets you touch another continent,
sets up a friendship that will last you all your lives

though you do not write or speak yet of the war's dark spaces –
your mother's death; the false wall in the Dutch boy's home
behind which a Jewish girl took refuge.

You're moving out into a peaceful future: white doves
holding olive branches, and the flags of all the world
flapping together on the shores of Lake Geneva.

You travel and learn languages, speak Esperanto
('the hoping one'), have faith in ecumenism,
the United Nations, the World Peace Jamboree,

the end of empire, new countries, new constitutions,
buildings made of glass and steel displacing bombsites.
This energy, this sense of hope – the World Fair,

the Festival of Britain – is what propels you forward,
it never tarnishes, you don't grow cynical with age.
Instead, you're learning hospitality and lovingkindness,

things that will not sour. This, and a gentle politics
shared with your old pen-pal. Go forward sixty years
since you first met: you're dying, and the Dutchman

has Alzheimer's. But look how May-time recollects your lives:
all its lush growth and hopefulness, the new beech leaves
soft as cloth, the way they flutter in the breeze like flags.

Rummers and ladels

How close I might have come once, as a child,
to touching, in my granny's sideboard
– place of peppery smells and lining paper,
stoppered bottles of gold and scarlet liquids –
a crystal tumbler from which Sir Walter Scott
sipped whisky. Perhaps I fingered the rim of it,
made the crystal sing. Or were the glasses
that he drank from long since broken?

No one ever spoke of them. There's only
the story, in my grandfather's notebook from the twenties.
His mother tells it him, he gives it a title, writes it in her voice:
I think we should put our Rummers and Ladels
in the Plate Cupboard. You know Sir Walter Scott
probably drank his toddies from one or more of those.

She tells how Sir Walter once stayed for a week
at the home of Provost Marney of Arbroath,
and that the rummers he drank from were passed down
to the provost's spinster daughters. They gave them to their niece,
a Mrs Mitchell, who'd a brother, *not exactly daft, but just a little queer,*
and bedridden. And on Sunday afternoons, *my father went up*
to give him the news and especially to tell all the jokes he had heard.
So Mrs Mitchell *was very good to us,* and *when she heard*
we had no ladels, she brought us Provost Marney's
together with the crystal glasses from which Sir Walter sipped.

The marks Scott's lips made on the glasses were washed away
two hundred years ago by Provost Marney's servant girl.
But still, if I were to hold one of those rummers, and drink from it
a shot of malt, would some sense of him imbue me?
Illogical as kissing bones of saints, but there's potency
in relics. Even the notebook telling the story has become one:
I turn the soft cream pages with their copperplated ink, fondling
this meagre piece of history. It's as though we dip our hands
into the huge dark bran tub of the past, grateful for anything we find:
this sliver that will flow on through our family like a ballad.

The coevals

There's something strange about the stars
this week of 1882, late winter easing into spring:
something lighting on two babies being born

across the sea from one another. The girl-child's
born in London: seven maids run up and down
six flights of stairs with jugs of water, scuttlefuls of coal.

The boy-child's born in Dublin, into a household
slipping into debt and moonlight flits.
Both of them plunge into language:

up to their necks in it, playing about in it,
reading whatever comes into their hands.
Then beginning to write. Gawkily at first,

then stories come, and novels – and each one
cracks the spines of old Victorian books, loosens pages
from their bindings, rewrites everything,

makes narrative new – look, a whole book happens
on a single day – and each one expands, pulls out as if were
toffee, the sentence, and fills it with new-minted words.

Their books inhabit the cities they were born in,
they walk their characters down streets that they know
as well as they know their own skin.

They are presences to one another,
although they never meet: he reads her books,
she reads his *with spasms of wonder* –

she, the nightingale whose song's as sweet
and pure as the sounds of ancient Greek;
he, the yellow blackbird of his favourite Irish air.

Wartime. Her London home is blitzed,
she lives in terror of air raids, invasion.
He, half blind, in exile, will never go home.

It's 1941, late winter easing into spring.
Death eyes them both. He's first to go.
She follows, lets the river take her there.

They each have had their vision:
remade the vessel into which the story's
poured. The altered stars resume their course.

Letter to Katherine Mansfield

on having her portrait rejected by the National Portrait Gallery, 1933

But you look great, Katherine, in your red dress
with your hair as black as the sea at night
when you peered from the deck on the long journey north
and your eyes so dark and serious, unflinching

in the soft Cornish light that falls on you
as you sit in her studio only months before your death.
Already your eyes are shadowed, your skin so pale
and, under the vermilion of your dress, your lungs disintegrating.

Flowers surround you, golds and pinks, scarlet poppies,
creamy whites like the blossoms of the pear tree in your story.
Your cheeks and mouth are cherry red, there is so much red,
there is also blood red. She pitches you onto the canvas,

this artist, she makes you flame from it, there is no
ignoring you, wild colonial girl. But your reds are too bright
for the committee of the gallery who suggest perhaps
a pencil drawing? It's this or nothing say your friends.

So the portrait languishes, unseen. Fifty years on,
I'm sitting in a garden of frost and sunlight
reading your letters and journals in a book on whose cover
is that portrait, staring up at me, showing me a writer's life.

Years later, I will give birth to a daughter
and name her for the girl in your stories, the girl they say
is like you, the sparky one, the curious one,
the one who rolls in the grass and goes where she shouldn't.

Still not in the gallery, Katherine, but here among us,
your character's name on our lips, your stories read over and over,
and you in that picture, defiant and vibrant, your reds
like the petals of tulips, crimson in winter.

A language of flowers

The child in the field is splitting stalks with her thumbnail
and threading flowers through the slits she's made

like the girl five hundred years before her, singing
dayseye, dayseye as she loops the string around her neck

in exactly the same way as the girl, a thousand years earlier,
who's running home through a white-speckled field

letting the name her mother taught her,
dæges eage, dæges eage, thrum in her head.

*

The bees go right inside these speckled flowers
and so do her fingers, fitting perfectly into the tips

just like the paws of the redbrown fox, creeping out
at night, wearing his purple *foxes glofa*.

*

Here in the cow pasture, she finds the yellow flowers
that grow by the slops, *cusloppe, cusloppe*,

and clutches a bunch of them, round as the sun,
and the girl a few centuries after her

goes cowslipping, makes balls for playthings,
strips petals for wine – *cowslips* so commonplace,

part of her parlance, she never dreams of a time
when a child won't know their name.

A gift of wildflowers

i.m. Esme, 2006–2007

From the summer hedgerow, a briar rose,
its golden froth of stamen, white petals
touched with pink: this for a memory
of her naming day of sun and wind,
pinks and whites, her rosebud dress –

and from Deepdale wood, this last cranesbill,
bright pink among the dank black leaves,
tiny veined petals so fragile it seems a breath
would loosen them and they would fall,
a scattering of stars inside the darkest place.

Diptych

after Celia Paul

She has sat here for so many hours,
her back to the wall, her skirts

spreading out on the floor, her presence
in the studio so familiar

that when it's all over, the portrait complete
and she's no longer here

it seems that the space still contains her
and so the artist paints her absence

– the same rug she sat on, the floorboards,
the skirting boards' lines, the wall

where her shadow fell – the place
she once inhabited so thick with light

that it feels tangible,
the sitter's figure palpable

in the same way that God is implied
in portraits where the painted light

falls from a window
transfiguring a face;

in the same way that after a death
a ghost may be see as a haze or a flare.

So in the diptych of presence and absence
a woman is painted: here, in this picture,

her flesh and her dress; and in this one
her still-present spirit, its portrait.

Moon over Catterline

'She [the painter Joan Eardley] loved the poetry of John Clare.'
Margot Sandeman

Almost a hundred years after his death, the ghost of John Clare
visits Catterline, where a woman stands in a field, painting it,
painting it, pressing the grasses and flowerheads into the paint.

Wind flows through Clare like thread through a needle. He gapes
at the drop of cliffs: it's as if he stood at the top of the church tower.
He's seen tides on the Thames, but never such a drag and rush
as this, and the vastness of water – he thought a fishpond
Paradise, can hardly comprehend this endless, restless ocean.

He watches as the painter takes out chalks and sketchbook now,
sets to drawing stalks of barley. He remembers he always had
some sly slip of paper about him, a pencil stub, noting things down.
We are the same, he thinks, so little divides us, only time and place,
the customs of our age. And he leans against her, back to back,
so she feels something propping her, airy and solid, like the wind.

She's taken a book from her knapsack, an old battered copy
of Clare – what made her pick up this one from the shelf?
She likes the way he talks of maple trees, their bark like corduroy,
of a robin's *olive feathers,* a ladybird *in the cowslip pips;*
how he knows certain fields as well as he knows his own heart.

As she does: *Once I start in a place, I find I don't want to move.*
The more I know the particular spot, the more I find to paint.

Helpston and Catterline, he wants to tell her, we make them new:
look at this breaking wave, this grass-blade, beetle, fox-fern, primrose –

*

Late afternoon, and he follows her past the rickety beehives.
Faint as the smell of honey in a cloverfield, he remembers
shapes of hives and the little worlds inside the skeps,
the inmates buzzing, asylums of bees.

A line of washing's flying back and forth, white sheets
in a billow of light and air. What Patty would have given
for drying winds like these –

                        Neighbours call to each other
and he no more understands their talk than they would his.
So let the country be divided, let there be different tongues,
we are none the worse for it, the language is made manifold.
In my father's house there are many mansions: in each one,
a different way of flexing words through mouth and breath.

He slips with the painter inside her cottage, which is not
so very different from his own – earth floor, makeshift ceiling.
She sits with her book, and a mug of tea. Then glances up
and sees him clear: but isn't frightened, he's dapper and polite,
he nods and smiles, he does not wish to startle her.
He's wearing gaiters and a waistcoat, looks Victorian. His face
is kind and smiling, as if, like the angels, he's saying, 'Be not afraid.'

She supposes he's the ghost of someone who once lived here,
then left for Aberdeen or Stonehaven, came back with fine clothes.
Though when she looks at his boots she sees they're worn through,
as though he has walked many miles.

She wonders what he makes of the sailcloth on the ceiling,
the paints and brushes in the sink. But he doesn't seem surprised,
and when he – falteringly – speaks, she knows he's not from here:
the accent's more Sussex, where she lived as a child
before the war, in the days of cows, her father's dairy farm.

That's where the voice reminds her of, when he says,
'We are comfortable here, are we not?' and she nods,
too taken aback for speech. His hands are like her father's,
worn and rough from the land, or like the hands
of the fishermen whose nets she paints.

As suddenly as he appeared and spoke, he's gone.
But she hears the sudden clatter of a palette falling from the sink,
the rattle of paintbrushes in a jar, which cannot be the wind.

It's only when words from the book she's been reading
– *the grass below* – *the vaulted sky* – come into her head
that she suddenly knows who he is, or was: John Clare.

*

Later, she goes out to watch the evening light, its fall on waves,
the pale moon rising over Catterline. He understands this,
he knows how it is, endlessly seeing the same place on earth.
John Clare, walking and walking the parish of Helpston.

Wandering the cliffpath, she feels something touch her,
soft as the brush of barley on her hand. Is his ghost still here?

She goes to her work, left out in the field, sees what's been blown
onto wet oil paint: seedheads, grains of sand. And in this corner,
a tiny fleck of red – a ladybird. *Clock-a-clay,* he called it.
She prises it off with her fingernail, and while she's wondering
if it's damaged, it lifts its wings and flies from her, out into the dusk.

Making the moon jar

To make a jar as perfect as those from the Choson dynasty
– enormous rounded vessels used for storing grains of rice –
the potter must learn patience. Over and over again,
what emerges from the kiln is cracked or buckled, weak
at the circumference. Another one, flawed and unglazed,
heaved onto the truck, taken down the track into the woods,
where she smashes raw white pottery to bits and buries it.
Back in the studio, her hands shape into being two new hemispheres,
slippery as newborns. She balances one onto the other, smoothes
wet clay between them, makes them whole. First firing, no cracks yet –
she dips the vessel in a milky glaze. Another firing, then
the opening of the kiln-mouth, the lifting out: a full moon jar.
She moves around it, strokes the pearly skin of porcelain,
feels the slight ridge round the centre, an equator. Two halves
are joined. Her heart is singing at what her hands have made.

The brightest star

(Henrietta Swan Leavitt, 1868–1921)

Is it because she can hear nothing that she strains her eyes
to see the farthest stars? Her ears blur sound
but her eyes look through the thirteen lenses
layered inside this telescope she's invented;
her eyes see all the known stars of the universe
and she's the one who starts recording them.

Her mind – the brightest one in Harvard, so they say –
works out a way of knowing how far away
a star is from the earth: by calculating brightness,
she can measure distance. Because of this,
they start to map out space: to calibrate
how big the Milky Way is, how old the universe.

She finds new stars – novae that suddenly
shine bright, then fade away. Cancer eclipses her.
By the time they think of her for the Nobel, she's dead.
Instead they name a crater on the moon for her.
The maps of galaxies go on and on expanding.
She's watching from a soundless place, light years ahead.

Mozart's requiem

Your last day on earth: Vienna in winter.
Snow on the streets, the river frozen.
You're thirty-five. Inside your house,
a fire is lit, your friends have arrived
to practice this mass you're composing.
Four of you, a part each, the voices
flying in and out of one another,
the way geese in flight pattern the sky.
The whole house filled with singing.
It drifts outside like chimney-smoke.

You stop to rest: your voice is weak,
your body sick these past few months.
The maid brings schnapps and coffee,
has sent out for pastries, crumbling
warm and soft in the mouth. Dusk
comes early, almost the solstice.
They close the shutters. *One more time,
let's sing it through again.* This requiem
you're writing for someone else's death.
Your tears fall as you sing, and later

they will say that this was premonition.
Perhaps they felt it too – Franz, Josepha,
Benedikt – whose clear true voices
were the first to sing *The Magic Flute,*
who are singing with you now,
encircling you with song. It's grown dark,
already evening. Your strength is gone.
The others leave, go out into the snow.
From the street they'll see that tiny crack
of light where the shutters barely close.

Your last sweet afternoon on earth.
Hold to this in your feverish sleep –
a room with firelight and candlelight,
food and drink, a circle of voices
singing your requiem mass. Hold to this
next day as the solitary gravedigger
hacks the frozen ground to make
your unmarked grave. Hold to this,
and watch how the geese mark the sky
as they fly the breadth of the world.

A homecoming

i.m. Duncan Glen

'and a forekent intelligence of licht / explodes the sadness'
from 'Amethyst', Duncan Glen

As if the ward were an underworld – no daylight, no fresh air,
one small window onto a courtyard, no telling where the sun
would rise or set – and leaving it an entry back up to the earth;
earth with its soft September light, its lovely – even in the carpark –
lungfuls of air, green of the field by the roundabout, newly yellowed leaves.

And home – being home felt like being held in light, the way the windows,
facing east and west, fill the room with it. Gazing out at trees,
drinking tea of fresh lemonbalm my sister's made, while my daughter
shows me words in her new dictionary; eating home-made food
round a table with a family – things that have become extraordinary.

Or, in the afternoon, to sit on the garden bench – the last of the roses,
the washing blowing on the line, a basket of windfalls, the autumn air.
And so on, through this day where everything is brushed with newness,
miracle; a sense of light and lightness, a kind of gentleness –
and Duncan, I'm wondering now if this was what surrounded you

that same day in late September, when both of us shifted from one world
to another. Your damaged body, held by those who love you,
grown weightless, *near translucent*, maybe, as you saw your father
when he drew close to death. And then the spirit lifting
from the tired, failed flesh, taken off into another element –

not rowed into a dark cave by some hooded figure, but carried
in a vessel filled with light and air, like a white-sailed felucca
on the Nile. Both of us released that day, into life, into an afterlife.
Death and rebirth, the oldest story; pomegranate seeds
brought out of darkness, a glistening handful –

but again, I come back to the way you wrote of your father,
singing as he tended his chrysanthemums
though he knew he wouldn't live to see them flower;
and it's how I see you too, tending to poetry, the song going on,
things still coming into bloom, long after this long day has ended.

Holy water

The Dark Ages: a ship sails into the Firth of Clyde, bearing its freight
of sacred earth from the Holy Land, brought back to consecrate
a Scottish church. But it's blown off course, the cargo's lost,
plummeting down to the bottom of a sealoch, which is, by this accident,
made holy, given its name. Centuries pass. The wrecked ship rots,
the holy soil blurs into sediment. Then come the submarines,
ominous heads looming out of the loch, hulls bloated with missiles.
In the USSR, an elderly priest is remembering how,
each January, he'd lead his congregation to a lake,
crack a hole in the ice and dip his wooden cross into the water.
So the whole lake was blessed, everyone filled vessels with this liquid,
exorcised, made incorruptible, and took it home to bless their food,
their drink, to sprinkle on their children as they left the house.
The people's memories of rituals like this have been submerged
through all the years of communism, but he remembers,
he wants to perform it again, the Great Blessing of the Water.

Years pass. The Cold War is over. The warheads
are gone from the loch, its surface unblemished once more.

The days are beginning, just slightly, to lighten. The priest
gathers a crowd of believers, goes to the lakeshore
and does what he's dreamt of for so many years.
A body of water blessed and made holy: a symbol,
he tells them, of the sanctity of all creation, of all the water
patterning the globe and flowing round it. Follow a river
as it thaws, out towards the sea, the Baltic, the North Sea,
the Atlantic, let the wind take you up this rivermouth,
this sealoch, and air fill your lungs as you plunge
down to the silt, its sacred grains of earth
contaminated now by leaking debris

from the submarines. Then come up from the deep
of Holy Loch, up through its altered particles
of water – the tainted and the sanctified –
until you break the surface and emerge,
the drops of liquid falling from your hallowed skin.

In the city, she thinks of Beauty Creek

She's never seen the place in winter: it's like trying to picture
a child being old, it can scarcely be done. Mud frozen,
falls stopped: sheen of ice over rocks. Rush and tumble of streams
halted and silent. Lakes enamelled with ice. Land under snow,
bound with it, bandaged. Bulbs and roots fixed in stiff earth,
the whole landscape suspended, in stasis: like someone near death
who has no energy for anything but breathing. Even the bears
are asleep in their caves. Even the river, the great pale green
Sunwapta, is ice, is still. This is the hardest thing to imagine,
like thinking of the dead. And the house by the river,
its spring-water frozen, windows curtained with snow
making a strange underwaterish light in the rooms
where everything will be as she left it: the woodpile, the table,
pots by the stove, the gleaming jars of bottled fruit,
dark gold of maple syrup she drew out from the trees.
A house with no one in it, like a body emptied of its soul.
Everything closed down, closed in on itself. As if,
when she left, she were Persephone, and in her absence,
winter came. As if she'd turned the huge Sunwapta into ice.
Something must make it happen, something mythical
that would make you believe in what's unseen –
a house under snow with its bottles and jars,
the pent force of a stopped river, and underneath the ice
six feet of air, and down below that, water still flowing,
the silty, unstoppable water with its living fish.

His resurrection

'all should know that I have not died'
Federico García Lorca

They say the resurrection happened in a garden,
so let your mutilated body find itself here,
among fountains and white irises and orange trees,
where a woman, saying your name under her breath,
will come upon you. *Yes*, you'll say to her, *it's true*,
and you'll reach for an orange fallen on the dusty ground
and open it and give her half. She'll suck the sweet juice,
spit the pips into her palm, keep them to plant
on that pit of bones, your unmarked grave.

And if resurrection happened on a country road, let it be here,
on the white track over the mountains, alongside your friends
heading out of the city. They're scared of you, stranger,
afraid you'll denounce them for talking of the poet's murder,
can't help themselves, can't stop thinking of you.
At the next village, something compels them, they ask you
into the inn, offer you bread, wine, olives. It's when
your own poetry spills from your lips that they know you:
embrace you, pour more wine, hold you tighter –

And if it happened by a lake, why not here? Pale turquoise water
lapping on sand, young boys cooking fish on a fire. They feed you
and the soft flesh breaks in your fingers, falls from the bones.
Or if the risen body can appear on a hillside, let it be here
where tiny blue candles of hyacinths grow out of the grass,
and let the season be spring, not the hot August day
when they shot you, but now, with the warm April wind
and the almonds in blossom, when out of the rockface
come the new leaves of fig trees, a luminous green.

And if it takes place inside, in an upper room, let it be this one,
where squares of sunlight fall through open shutters
and the man who lives here comes to you, lifts your white shirt
with its bloodstains, touches the tender places where the bullets
split your flesh; and then you'll sit together looking out
across the olive groves, and he'll bring you honey cakes,
water fresh from the spring. *Here, companero*, he'll say,
take it, eat and drink – and you'll show him how the resurrection
works, put the words of your poems into his mouth.

This life

After the endless journey in airless heat
you emerge at last from the underground
and here at the newsagent's next to the station
are bunches of sweet peas, wrapped in pink tissue:

you buy some, and bury your face as you walk,
sun and wind on your skin, in butterfly petals,
pale pinks and lilacs, white, their summer smell –
as if you were returning from the underworld

to find the meadows blossoming once more.
Each life echoing, acting out these myths:
going into darkness, re-emerging, wounds
and griefs healed over, the luscious world

still there, offering itself up to us over and over
again; not an afterlife, not something dangled
in the future – those fields of asphodel – with absences,
abstractions, but this life with its city streets,

its fizz and mix and mess, its rush of sweet-pea scent,
the lightness of their petals, their brief and lovely bloom.

Elizabeth Burns has published three previous collections of poetry, including *Ophelia and other poems* (Polygon, 1991), which was short-listed for a Saltire Award for First Book of the Year. Her work has appeared in many anthologies, including *The Faber Book of Twentieth Century Scottish Poems* and Canongate's *Modern Scottish Women Poets*. Elizabeth Burns has spent much of her life in Scotland, and now lives in Lancaster, where she teaches creative writing.